**Deeper Encoun**

C000136380

# SLOW TO ANGER

John Wilks

7 studies for leaders of confident small groups
with CD audio tracks and photocopiable worksheets

DEEPER ENCOUNTER: SLOW TO ANGER by John Wilks

Scripture Union, 207–209 Queensway, Bletchley, MK2 2EB, UK
email: info@scriptureunion.org.uk
www.scriptureunion.org.uk

Scripture Union Australia: Locked Bag 2, Central Coast Business Centre, NSW 2252
www.su.org.au

ISBN 1 84427 171 4

First published in Great Britain by Scripture Union 2006

Scripture quotations, unless otherwise indicated, are taken from the Holy Bible, New International Version. Copyright © 1973, 1978, 1984 by International Bible Society. Anglicisation copyright © 1979, 1984, 1989. Used by permission of Hodder and Stoughton Limited.

British Library Cataloguing-in-Publication data: a catalogue record for this book is available from the British Library.

Cover design by mhm grax of London

Internal page design by Creative Pages: www.creativepages.co.uk

Printed and bound by goodmanbaylis, The Trinity Press, Worcester and London

Scripture Union is an international Christian charity working with churches in more than 130 countries providing resources to bring the good news about Jesus Christ to children, young people and families – and to encourage them to develop spiritually through the Bible and prayer. As well as co-ordinating a network of volunteers, staff and associates who run holidays, church-based events and school Christian groups, Scripture Union produces a wide range of publications and supports those who use their resources through training programmes.

## FOREWORD

'... *a unique, insightful and imaginative resource which will help satisfy a growing hunger among mature Christian people ... a series that will nourish serious disciples in our churches.'*

If we want to be people who live out our Christian faith with integrity in a complex world, we need to be people who are serious in our engagement with God's word – following the example of the early church seekers and disciples who 'every day ... studied the Scriptures' and were 'devoted to the apostles' teaching'.

The great thing about the *Deeper Encounter* series is that it is a stimulating resource honed to fulfil these aims. Challenging central themes about the nature of God and the way of salvation have been selected. We are encouraged to relate the focal passages to both their scriptural and historical contexts. Our individual Christian journeys are properly affirmed and we are encouraged to integrate these with Scripture – yet Scripture is not sacrificed on the altar of the personal or the contemporary. The mix of printed text, audio input via CD and worksheets means that interest is sustained and stimulated.

This is a series that will nourish serious disciples in our churches, enabling us to respond by informing our minds with God's truth, opening our hearts to God's light, shaping our wills by God's ways, and above all learning to relate more deeply to who God is – his character as revealed in Scripture.

**The Rev Dr David Spriggs**
Head of Church Relations, Bible Society

## Welcome!

This series of small group studies is particularly aimed at confident small groups: groups of about 6 to 12 people who have a good general grounding in Bible knowledge and who are ready for a more demanding study with searching questions. In fact, the quality of the interactive question times is one of the strong distinctives of the *Deeper Encounter* series. This feature will appeal to groups who have grown tired of more predictable question and answer sessions and need to move on to the kind of discussion that leaves everyone stimulated and energised.

Each of these seven studies follows a flexible pattern that will be described in the Introduction that follows. Integral and vital to the studies is the extra material on the CD. Three clips are to be played at the appointed times during each session. They provide valuable width to the study, and I trust will also give real enjoyment.

Although not spoken by the author but by a professional actor, the CD tracks will enable the groups to experience a level of relationship with John Wilks through his words which I know will be one of the rewarding aspects of the material. John is Director of Open Learning at the London School of Theology (formerly London Bible College) and his experience makes him the ideal writer of material for a group that wants to go deeper into the biblical material and with a strong focus on application. He has an impressive ability to be very challenging in the area of application – beyond the obvious! And he brings a creativity and liveliness to the study not always found in theological material! John is married to Joanne and together they have seven children, ranging from early twenties to five years old. He is the pianist and one of the preachers at a community church they helped to establish in 1991. I know you will enjoy getting to know him through these studies.

If you benefit from this study I hope you will move on to others in the series. Details of other titles are given at the back of the book.

You will have noticed that the series is branded with the logo of *Encounter with God*, a quarterly personal Bible reading guide publication from Scripture Union which it is my privilege to edit. *Deeper Encounter* is aimed at the same kind of readership as *Encounter with God*, so if you have gained from using this material in a small group you are warmly invited to look at using the Bible reading guide to which it is a companion if you don't do so already. Again, you'll find full details at the back of this book.

Finally, it is often said that small group leaders are some of the unsung heroes of church life. The small group is where many people spend their most significant times around God's Word. We hope that *Deeper Encounter* will help you in your important task of communicating to them the truth and relevance of the Bible. May God's Spirit equip and enable you as you lead them through *Slow to Anger*.

**Andrew Clark**
Editor, *Encounter with God*

## Introduction: Slow to Anger

A major aim of this *Deeper Encounter* study booklet is that our spirituality, our personal relationship with God, will deepen and grow. This book will study a classic Old Testament phrase. On nine separate occasions, God is said to be 'slow to anger'. This saying became very important for the way the Israelites thought about God, and the way they wrote about him. It appears in several psalms, a variety of the prophets and in a number of different narrative books.

This small group study will look at eight of these passages. It will show that this is not a 'throw away' phrase dreamt up on a whim or on the spur of the moment. It became a recurring phrase, one the Israelites returned to on many occasions. Through the course of these study sessions, we will find a consistent pattern: it is part of their standard description of the God they got to know over the centuries. When they wanted to know what their God was like, one of the things they would remind themselves of was that he was slow to anger. We can benefit enormously from learning why they wanted to do that.

Each of these seven studies follows a flexible pattern. There is a **Leader's briefing** which is designed to equip group leaders to approach the session and should not be read to the group; and there are interactive question sections under the possible headings of **Orientation** (context setting), **Investigation, Evaluation** and **Application**. The last three of these are discussion times prompted by questions, and these questions are repeated (without leader's notes) on the **Photocopiable worksheets** at the back of the book. As leader you can decide whether to give out these worksheets in advance or at the beginning of each session. Some groups will be very ready to do a little 'homework' in preparation for the session; others may find this commitment too much of a burden.

In addition, there are audio tracks from the CD for each session. The **Introduction** track is mainly scene setting; the **Observation** track will give extra insights and reflections from my own experience; the **Summary** will highlight the major points of the session.

Whenever I make reference to something in one of the audio tracks – be it to a Bible verse, a song, hymn or film, or an individual from history – you will find the reference included in the book. Hopefully this means that you are fully equipped to answer questions.

Each session concludes with a brief and optional **Adoration** section. Your knowledge of your group will help you to decide which, if any, elements of prayer and worship would be appropriate to close the session; I have opted not always to be too specific about hymns or songs because of the wide range of churchmanship of the groups using the material. But you will find some suggestions to use or to adapt.

## Contacting me

If you want to, you can contact me in one of two ways.

- Visit my blog on http://homepage.mac.com/wilksenterprise/blogwavestudio/index.html.
- Send an email to wilksenterprise@mac.com

On the blog you will find live links for all the Internet links mentioned in this book, as well as any updates on that information. You'll hear me describing the process of writing further books, and have the opportunity to comment on that process. In addition, you will be able to let me know how your sessions went, and pass on any encouragements or frustrations you have found. Finally, there is information not only about *Deeper Encounter* but also about other aspects of my work and interests. I cannot guarantee to respond to every email or comment personally, but certainly look forward to hearing your input.

**John Wilks**

# Contents

**Please note:** All worksheet pages at the back of this book are photocopiable; alternatively, they are accessible as PDF files from the audio CD for you to print out locally.

# 1: MOUNTAIN TOP ENCOUNTER

**EXODUS 34:6**

## Leader's briefing

We begin with two closely connected studies looking at narratives from the Pentateuch. In this session we will be looking at Exodus 34; in the next session at Numbers 14. In both, the description of God as 'slow to anger' is incorporated in a number of other statements. It could easily get overlooked. It is, however, an incredibly positive character trait. Ordinarily, if we characterise someone's temper, we refer to their 'quick' temper. To register that someone is *slow*-tempered is not so common, and to say so on repeated occasions is an indication of how important this is.

Our key phrase is not the only positive thing that this passage has to say about God; it occurs in a setting of other exceptionally encouraging character traits, any one of which could be the subject of in-depth study. Only constraints on your study time would give you any reason for restricting discussion of the other phrases around it. They add together to give a clear picture of how great our God is!

Yet, while the description of God's personality emphasises some extremely positive attributes, the picture emerging towards the end of verse 7 is somewhat darker. We will not look at this aspect in any depth during this session; that is the task for the next session. For the moment, we focus on establishing a wider context for the key phrase that forms the backbone of our study.

One feature of these first two sessions is the need to establish the context for each reading. This could result, however, in the temptation to focus on the wider context. Certainly there are questions that could be raised by trying to make a more explicit connection between the Golden Calf incident in Exodus 32 and the passage under consideration in Exodus 34. There are a few optional questions set if you feel the group would want to focus on this aspect and accept the challenge of dealing with the implications. In the main, however, the study will focus on the set passage.

## Preparation

**Play** CD track 1. It's unlikely that there will be questions arising from the audio track, so you can probably move straight to the reading.

**Read** Exodus 34:1–9 (or 33:12 – 34:9 if you want a better sense of the background).

## Orientation

Establish the context for this reading by looking back in Exodus. Each group will need to decide for itself just how far back in Exodus it needs to go to establish the context for the reading. If everyone has already had and worked through their photocopied sheets, then you might prefer to skip this bit. A good point to start from would be Exodus 32, but you might prefer to go back as far as Exodus 19. Let the group flick though the pages of their Bible as you provide a brief overview covering these main points:

| | |
|---|---|
| Exodus 19 | The Israelites arrive at Mount Sinai; Moses makes several trips up the mountain, preparing the people to receive God's message. |
| Exodus 20 | The Ten Commandments are given. |
| Exodus 20:22 – 23:19 | The 'Book of the Covenant', the core portion of Torah, elaborates on the central commandments. |
| Exodus 24 | Further narrative description of events around the mountain experience between God and Moses. |
| Exodus 25 – 31 | Construction plans for the tabernacle. |
| Exodus 32:1–6 | Aaron makes the golden calf. |
| Exodus 32:7–14 | God sends Moses down the mountain; Moses successfully pleads with God not to destroy the people. |
| Exodus 32:15–20 | Moses arrives in the camp, destroying the two tablets of the covenant. |
| Exodus 32:21–29 | Moses takes punishment into his own hands, ordering the Levites to kill the worst offenders. |
| Exodus 32:30–35 | Moses asks for forgiveness for the people. |
| Exodus 33:1–11 | God withdraws from the people, but establishes a tent of meeting with Moses. |
| Exodus 33:12 – 34:9 | Moses asks for – and receives – a further revelation of God's identity and character. |
| Exodus 34:10–28 | A summary of the covenant. |

If the group want to ask questions about these events, then you need to be aware that there is nothing here to help you! Our interest is Exodus 34, not Exodus 19–33.

Your quick trip through Exodus should establish the following :

- The two stone tablets (Exodus 34:1) are replacements for the ones Moses smashed (Exodus 32:19).
- God's proclamation of his character is part of his revelation of himself as his goodness passes in front of Moses.

The larger context is the narrative of the golden calf, and the punishment that followed it.

## Investigation

1 How do you feel as you read God's self-description in Exodus 34:6,7?

2 Which part of the statement particularly resonates with you?

3 Are you surprised to discover that the Old Testament describes God as 'slow to anger'? Does this fit your perception of God? Of the Old Testament?

4 Which would you find most encouraging to your faith: a glimpse of God's glory (Exodus 33:18,23) or insight into an abstract theological statement of God's character (Exodus 34:6,7)? Why?

5 So why does God explain himself in both ways?

6 In Numbers 12:8 (among other places) we are told that Moses spoke with God 'face to face'. Exodus 33:20 states that even Moses cannot see God's face and live. How can this be consistent?

**Note:** To give you a hint at the answer here, the phrase 'face to face' appears to refer to an especially direct communication. We would use the phrase to mean a personal meeting, rather than over the phone, for instance. In the context of the Old Testament it means that Moses did not need an intermediary to speak with God on his behalf. The Israelites would have expected priests and prophets to be representatives or mediators; as the intermediary, Moses was not in need of one himself.

### Optional extra questions

The following questions attempt to connect between chapters 34 and 32 of Exodus. Feel free to omit these questions if you want to, or are running short of time. The **Observation** track will not make mention of these questions.

7 In Exodus 32:9-13, Moses narrowly averts God's anger erupting against the people. Does this somehow invalidate the statement that God is 'slow to anger'? How do we maintain a coherent and rational statement about God's character?

8 Looking at his actions in Exodus 32:19,20 and 32:25–28, would it be fair to say that Moses is 'slow to anger'? Does this affect our understanding of God as the one who is slow to anger?

**Note**: I am very struck by the anger Moses displays. Smashing the stone tablets was a very dramatic showdown; and if that was all he had done we might simply have said that 'his bark was worse than his bite'. But then he organises a slaughter of the worshippers. This might not have wiped out all the Israelites (see God's words in Exodus 32:10) but it was a significant number of people. So I wonder if we are meant to notice that God was slow to anger and open to a reasoned argument, while Moses' anger was sustained. Moses was not able to control his anger in the way that God controlled his.

## Observation

**Play** CD track 2. Give the group an opportunity to ask questions to clarify what they have heard. Since the audio track does not introduce new material or ideas, there are no **Evaluation** questions for this session. When the group is ready, move on to **Application**.

**Texts mentioned**:

– 'Blessed are those who have not seen and yet have believed' John 20:29.

– 'Nothing's impossible I have found,
For when my chin is on the ground,
I pick myself up,
Dust myself off,
Start all over again.'

From the 1936 film *Swing Time*, lyrics by Dorothy Fields, music by Jerome Kern.

– 'When the dog bites,
When the bee stings,
When I'm feeling sad,
I simply remember my favourite things
And then I don't feel so bad.'

From the 1965 film *The Sound of Music*, lyrics by Oscar Hammerstein II, music by Richard Rodgers.

## Application

9 What would you include if asked to write your own 50-word description of God's character?

10 Looking at God's self-description in Exodus 34, would you have had a similar balance between 'positive' and 'negative' aspects of God's character?

11 If your summary would have been balanced differently, why?

12 Which parts of your description are based on a theological statement about God? Which parts relate to your own experiences of God?

13 What role (if any) do our past experiences of God play in forming our perception of who God is?

### Optional extra questions

If you attempted the optional questions in the **Investigation** section you might like to try the following:

14 To what extent should we emulate God as the One who is 'slow to anger'? Are we too much like Moses for it to be worth trying to develop a slow temper?

## Summary

**Play** the summary for this session on CD track 3.

## Adoration

Share together:

- past experiences of God's character
- songs or hymns which reflect on those experiences
- prayers of thankfulness

# 2: THE WHOLE WICKED COMMUNITY

**NUMBERS 14:18**

### Leader's briefing

In this second narrative from the Pentateuch, Numbers 14, our attention turns to the somewhat darker aspects of the passages. The description of God's character refers to him punishing sin, and of doing so for an extended period of time. Furthermore, in both narratives the people of God have fallen into serious corporate sin. While we can take encouragement from the statement that God does not have a hair-trigger temper liable to explode at the slightest provocation, the other side of the coin appears to be that when he acts to punish the guilty it will be comprehensive punishment.

An easily overlooked aspect of the passage is the fact that God does not punish absolutely everybody. He exempts two individuals, noting that they were faithful, trusting him in the face of the difficulties (Numbers 14:30). There is a reminder here that if we are corporately guilty, we are individually saved. The modern world would have it the other way round: individually punished and corporately (universally) saved.

This is not to deny the hugely difficult questions that remain. The passage implies that every single one of the Israelites rejected the pleading of Caleb, Joshua, Moses and Aaron. You may well be asked, how can this really include young children? While I want to affirm the importance of a democratic vote that allows each individual to have their say, I have to acknowledge that this is not what the Bible says; it was simply not their way of understanding the world. The head of the family alone had a vote – and the rest of the family accepted the way he (and it would always have been 'he') voted.

So the passage is saying that not one of those family heads voted with the leadership. The community came to a corporate decision, and all took the rewards or punishments equally.

This session brings a challenging topic to the fore of the discussion. It would be unwise to expect that such a difficult topic could be 'dealt with' in its entirety in a single session. But the group will begin to wrestle with the gap in cultures between the strong corporate identity of the Chosen People and the intense individualism of today's Western societies.

## Preparation

**Play** CD track 4.

**Read** Numbers 14:1–25 (or 14:10–23).

## Orientation

Establish the context for this reading by looking at earlier chapters of Numbers. The context should be much quicker to establish compared to the previous session. The group should not need to look any further back than chapter 13. As before, quickly flick through the chapters and note the following events:

| | |
|---|---|
| Numbers 13:1–20 | Choosing 12 explorers. |
| Numbers 13:21–25 | They go off to explore for 40 days. |
| Numbers 13:26–33 | When they return, their report stresses the difficulties. |
| Numbers 14:1–9 | The people declare it would be better if they had never left Egypt; Moses and Aaron plead with them not to respond in this way, but to trust in God. |
| Numbers 14:26–36 | God's condemnation of the people: 'this whole wicked community' (14:35). |

## Investigation

1  Are you shocked by the speed with which God declares his intention to punish the people (verses 11,12)?

2  In verses 17 and 18 we see Moses confront God with his own declaration about his character that we studied from Exodus 34. Which of the following do you think is the best explanation for what is going on here?

  – that God has forgotten how he is meant to behave and needs to be reminded? (In other words, if Moses had not said these things then God would have done what he declared he would do in verse 12.)

  – that God is testing Moses, to see if he has learnt what God's true character is like?

- that prayer can change how God acts?

- a subtle combination of these options?

3  How should we interpret the phrase 'punishes the children for the sin of the fathers to the third and fourth generation' (verse 18)?

**Note:** The **Observation** audio track which you will hear after this set of questions includes a response to this tricky question. In essence it says the following: the phrase is issued in the context of a society that put huge emphasis on the extended family. So it refers to the entire extended family standing there listening to Moses, including the grandchildren and great-grandchildren who happen to be alive at the time. The punishment is imposed on those alive at the time – not on those yet to be born. So the punishment does not extend endlessly. It is not a statement that punishment will simply continue on and on. Furthermore, it is applied to the sin of failing to trust God – failing to believe that he is capable of doing what he has promised to do – and not to any and every sin.

4  In Numbers 14:20, the Lord declares that he has forgiven the people. Nevertheless, the passage continues with the information that the people will be punished. Is this consistent?

5  Is there punishment for every sin we commit, even when we have asked for forgiveness? Or is this something that might only apply in certain situations?

6  What similarities can you find between the situation in Numbers 14 and that in Exodus 32?

**Note:** I am expecting some 'big picture' similarities here, not minute details. Perhaps the most obvious thing is that the people as a group fall into sin, and God reacts against that by threatening to destroy them. Moses pleads for them, and God makes a different decision.

7  What positive things can you spot in this passage, no matter how small they may be?

**Note:** As will be discussed further in the **Observation** audio track, God does not impose the punishment on Caleb and Joshua, the two spies who encouraged the people to put their trust in God and not to listen to the other spies. So, even though the entire population of the Israelite nation is treated as a single unit, the fact that these two individuals are separated out for different treatment is a reminder that God's judgement and punishment is not indiscriminate.

## Observation

**Play** CD track 5. Give the group a chance to ask any questions to clarify what they have heard and move on when ready.

**Texts mentioned:**

 – Abraham bargains with God over Sodom and Gomorrah – Genesis 18:20–33.

 – The 'plans to prosper you' – Jeremiah 29:11.

 – 'Showing love to a thousand generations of those who love me' – Exodus 20:5. This aspect is also in Exodus 34:7, though the idea of generations is not as strong.

## Evaluation

8   In the light of the punishment that results from the events surrounding these passages, is the claim that God is 'slow to anger' reasonable? Or empty and meaningless?

9   What is your reaction to the observation that it is in the context of such widespread sin that the affirmation of this particular side of God's character is made?

## Application

10   The sinful actions narrated in Exodus 34 and Numbers 14 are what we might call corporate sinfulness: the vast majority of the people fall into a sin. Are there any ways in which an entire local church can fall into corporate sinfulness?

11   In Numbers 14:11 and 14:23 God says that the people have treated him with contempt. What kind of thing might happen in a church today that might provoke God to view us in the same way, that we have treated him with contempt?

12   Are we – as Christians living after the crucifixion and the resurrection – somehow immune from punishment for such sin?

13   Are there occasions when we assume that our individual sinfulness warrants this level of response from God, even though it is nothing like the sort of sinfulness displayed by the Israelites?

14   What do these passages suggest about the contexts in which we might use such positive affirmations of God's character for ourselves?

15  What of relevance do we learn from these passages about the phrase 'slow to anger' and the contexts in which it is used?

## Summary

**Play** CD track 6.

## Adoration

Some suggestions for closing the session:

- Read 1 John 1:9 as a prelude to prayers of gratitude for God's forgiveness and cleansing.
- Re-read Jeremiah 29:11 and share in prayers of thankfulness for the way God has led his people in the past and of confidence in his future plans.
- Sing or say together any hymn or song which reflects on the cross and its work of forgiveness.

# 3: HELP AND COMFORT

## Leader's briefing

After examining two passages from the early narratives of the Old Testament, our attention now turns to the first of three psalms we will investigate in this series. This move from narrative to psalm will cause a significant shift in the content of the discussion. If previously we have looked at the way the phrase 'slow to anger' appears as part of a character statement for God and the way that it occurs in situations in which God's patience is being tested to the utmost, in this session we will be thinking about the way it affects how we pray and worship.

Discussion will probably cover two main areas: firstly, the extent to which we use familiar, even well worn and clichéd language, and the possible spiritual benefits of doing this; secondly, when and how we might incorporate lament into our services.

There are a number of implications to be drawn from the fact that the Israelites took up our key phrase 'slow to anger' and incorporated it into their worship. Questions may be raised about the potential insincerity of using phrases and images that appear so often that they become clichés. More positively, we are reminded of the huge spiritual benefits to be gained from turning to the familiar and the comfortable when we feel oppressed and troubled. The group will also want to think about the way that the use of general and non-specific language allows other people to take up a prayer and use it for themselves.

More significant than this, though, is the importance of gaining spiritual encouragement and comfort from the truth contained in our key phrase.

## Preparation

**Play** CD track 7.

**Texts mentioned:**

- The phrase 'my chains fell off' is from the hymn 'And can it be'.
- 'From all the perils of the night' is part of ancient church liturgies for evening prayer, vespers or compline.

- 'It's all about you' is from the Matt Redman song, 'I'm coming back to the heart of worship'.

**Read** Psalm 86

I recommend that the group try an antiphonal reading of the psalm. Either divide the group into two or choose a designated person (not necessarily you) to alternate with the rest of the group. The first line of each verse alternates with the rest of the verse. Note that verses 2, 9, 14, 16 and 17 each contain a trio of lines, so the responding group should read lines two and three.

## Investigation

1 Where and how do you imagine this psalm being used? Is it useful for congregational recitation? Or better used only by individuals?

2 Would you describe the imagery as innovative and creative? Or do you find it so full of stock phrases that you find it difficult to engage with? What are the implications of your verdict?

3 The psalmist spends more time praising God than talking about his problems. How realistic does this seem in the light of being 'poor and needy' (verse 1) and faced with 'the arrogant ... attacking' (verse 14)?

4 Who do you think are the 'arrogant', the 'band of ruthless men' and 'men without regard for you' (verse 14)? Do you need to identify them to be able to appreciate the psalm? Or is it actually better not to know?

## Observation

**Play** CD track 8. Give the group an opportunity to ask any questions to clarify what they have just heard; when they are ready, move on.

## Evaluation

5 Do you agree that in worship the familiar is encouraging and of greater comfort? Should worship make us feel comfortable?

6 Is our worship or prayer (private or corporate) made more or less meaningful by the use of stock phrases?

7 What other kinds of prayer can be meaningful and why?

## Application

8   How often do we make space in our services for lament? Is it
    something to reserve for challenging national and international
    situations, like the World Trade Centre attacks of 11 September
    2001, or the Indian Ocean Tsunami of Boxing Day 2004? Or
    something that should feature more regularly?

9   What spiritual benefit might there be from incorporating lament
    into our services? What would that mean? What would we want to
    lament to God about?

10  If this psalm models using general, non-specific terms to refer to a
    range of problems that people want to bring to God in prayer, can
    you come up with some contemporary parallel terms?

11  Do our prayers show the balance of praise and petition seen in
    this psalm? If not, why not?

## Summary

**Play** CD track 9.

**Texts mentioned:**

–   'trustworthy saying' – 1 Timothy 1:15; 3:1; 4:9; 2 Timothy 2:11;
    Titus 3:8

## Adoration

Some options for closing the session:

–   Prayerfully read Psalm 86 together. By all means use an antiphonal
    reading if the group is comfortable with the style, but at this point
    the emphasis should be on using the words as prayer, so
    experimentation is inappropriate. If the group accepts the idea
    that the familiar allows us to focus more on God, then ensure that
    the group is comfortable with what occurs.

–   In the light of the discussion, you may want to close your group
    time by singing one or two favourite and familiar worship songs or
    hymns chosen by group members.

# 4: AS FAR AS THE EAST IS FROM THE WEST

## PSALM 103

### Leader's briefing

Arriving at the midpoint of the study, we turn to what is, in my opinion, one of the most wonderful of all the psalms. It is my own favourite psalm; it contains distinctive and evocative imagery that should encourage us all. Its consistently positive and affirming portrayal of God and his love for his people makes it a text to which I constantly return.

The sheer exuberance of the psalm raises the question: on what basis can we be confident that this is an accurate description of God's character? Has the writer simply got so caught up with the subject that he's not ensuring that a rounded, balanced picture results?

The narrative passages in Exodus and Numbers we have looked at earlier in the series included other aspects of God's character – in particular, his punishment of sin. Here, such imagery is almost totally absent; we need to look hard for anything potentially negative!

In fact, I am convinced that there is every reason to be confident in the accuracy of the statements contained in this psalm; and that we can happily use them as the basis for theological descriptions of God's character. Giving space to a discussion of the questions should enable the group to come to the same sort of conviction and confidence.

One way of responding to this imagery is to create our own. Our creator God longs for us to respond creatively to him. To put these classic metaphors and ideas into contemporary terms is a way of honouring them while also reaching out to a twenty-first century world in images that will resonate with them as well. During this session, you will have the chance to consider some of my offerings, and for you and your group to make your own attempt at this. You should leave plenty of time for this exercise: 15 minutes at least.

Overall, the tone of this session should be positive. This is a rich, vibrant psalm. Hopefully, you will have fun writing new sayings to express these dynamic and vital truths about God's love and forgiveness.

**Note:** At the back of the booklet there is an extra photocopiable sheet for this session entitled **Exploring Psalm 103**. It is *not* intended to be given out in advance with the standard sheet of questions. Instead, it is intended to give out during the session itself if you feel that people will benefit from having a variety of ideas to work with as they formulate their rewritings of the text.

## Preparation

**Play** CD track 10.

**Read** Psalm 103. To add variety and in the light of the writing exercise in this session, why not use a paraphrase such as *The Message* or a contemporary Bible version such as the New Living Translation?

## Investigation

1   Psalm 103 uses a variety of images drawn from nature: from the height of the heavens to the fragility of desert grass. Which images particularly resonate for you, and why?

2   How much does this psalm rely on theologically sound statements in expressing God's character, and how much on poetic enthusiasm? Look, for example, at verse 10 and discuss its value. How far can we place our confidence in this and other verses in the psalm as objective truth to be trusted?

3   Is there anything here that hints at the same sort of balance of character traits of God used in the Exodus and Numbers passages we studied?

## Observation

**Play** CD track 11. Give the group an opportunity to ask questions to clarify what they have just heard. When ready, move on either to the **Evaluation** or to the **Application** questions.

**Texts mentioned:**

–   Various verses from Psalm 103; also verses studied earlier in Exodus 34:6,7 and Numbers 14:17,18.

–   'Showing love to a thousand generations of those who love me' – Exodus 20:5.

## Evaluation

4 Comparing Psalm 103:13,17; Exodus 34:7 and Numbers 14:18, do you agree that Psalm 103 gives a different perspective on the narrative texts? Is it correcting them, expanding on them, or realigning them towards something bigger? Or do you think something different is happening?

## Application

5 What alternative images can you think of to express in contemporary terms Psalm 103:11,12 (or Isaiah 1:18)? If the group has already looked at some different translations or paraphrases of the psalm, that will help them with their response to this question. Do they find the examples inspiring? Or do they want to reject them as being too colloquial or dated?

Here are a couple of my own attempts to use relevant imagery; and these are given as examples on the **Exploring Psalm 103** photocopiable sheet at the back:

- Though your sins be like motor-mechanic's fingers, they will be as clean as a newborn baby's.
- As thoroughly as Norton Utilities can securely wipe the information off your computer hard disk, so God has removed your sins from you.

You could also give the group some of the following situations with the invitation to use them as springboards for new sayings reminiscent of the psalm. Stress that there is no need to follow the 'as ..... as the ..... are...' structure. We can be more creative than that. It might help to break into smaller groups of twos and threes to discuss these together for five or ten minutes before sharing ideas as a whole group.

- Washing and cleansing imagery: showering, shampooing...
- Bathroom and kitchen cleanliness: detergents, disinfectants...
- Medical imagery: antibiotics, vaccines...
- Technology: transport, astronomy, computers...
- Extremities: uncrackable codes, immovable objects...
- Really dirty things: muddy sports kit, rust...
- Things we'd rather not touch: mouldy peaches, a takeaway curry dropped in the street...
- The mess only little children create: painting with all the drips, a full nappy...

When the group are sharing their ideas, the thing to watch out for is that they express the core idea correctly. Do they really express the way that God has totally forgiven us? Without appearing to criticise the author, it is still important to encourage evaluation on those lines.

6  How do you feel about this sort of exercise? Which suggestions for new images particularly resonate with you? Does it help you to appreciate the biblical text better?

7  Revelation 7:14 includes a somewhat bizarre image: robes washed in blood can come out white. What other ways are there of expressing the way that Jesus' death and resurrection has made forgiveness of sins possible?

8  For some people, the image of God as a 'celestial policeman' is a very dominant one. This psalm celebrates a picture of God that is virtually the exact opposite of that. How can we achieve a balanced view of God, a healthy picture encompassing his mercy and his judgement?

9  Compare the stock phrases of Psalm 86 with the creative imagery of Psalm 103. Which do you prefer and why?

## Summary

**Play** CD track 12.

**Texts mentioned:**

–  Micah 7:19

## Adoration

Some ideas to conclude this session:

–  Use your contemporary rewritings for meditative praying. You could have one person read the psalm very slowly, pausing after each verse, at which point anyone who had written an equivalent image could add it in.

–  Alternatively, use your contemporary rewritings to connect to the core phrase 'slow to anger'. For example:

> The Lord is slow to anger, abounding in love, for as thoroughly as Norton Utilities can securely wipe the information off your computer hard disk, so God has removed your sins from you.

# 5: THE GOD WHO RELENTS

## JONAH 4:2; NAHUM 1:3

### Leader's briefing

In this session our attention turns to two prophets who both had dealings with Nineveh, the capital city of the Assyrians. Nineveh occupied a distinctive position in the Israelite consciousness. The Assyrians were the nation that overran the northern kingdom Israel, and virtually annihilated Judah as well (2 Kings 17–19). Such events go deep into a nation's perception of itself and its history. To get an impression of that, we only need to think about the way that events of the Second World War have been recalled in Great Britain with their sixtieth anniversaries being marked over a number of years since the turn of the millennium.

Connecting up the Jonah of the book with the prophet mentioned in 2 Kings 14:25 would suggest that the events in the book of Jonah pre-date the fall of the northern kingdom, and possibly even the period when the Assyrians were a major power in the Ancient Near East. But after the event anyone reading the book of Jonah would readily have that in mind.

If Jonah is set in the period directly before the Assyrians rose to prominence, Nahum is set between the destruction of the northern kingdom and the southern kingdom (at the hands of the Babylonians). Politically, then, Assyria was at that point the local superpower, and responsible for the loss of the northern kingdom. There may have been little love lost between the two Israelite nations, but often it was more like the rivalry between siblings. The northern kingdom was not simply overrun, it was obliterated, and its people dispersed so widely that they were soon lost, not only to their Judean relatives but to history. Later prophets make passing allusion to these lost brethren, and the idea that they might return to Jerusalem, but the reality was that the people of the southern kingdom had no idea where they might be.

One potential red herring in any study on Jonah is the question of its historicity. Are these events that actually happened, or is this fiction with a moral intent – a parable to teach us something important? For the sake of this study, that is not a relevant question. Whatever the historicity, this is recorded in the Bible for the Israelites – and us – to learn from. More important to note is that Israelite prophets would not normally have travelled to the non-Israelite nations to deliver prophecies against them. Ordinarily, the audience for a prophecy such as Nahum were Israelites, not Assyrians. Furthermore, the intended audience for the written prophecies would have been Israelites, not Assyrians.

## Preparation 1

**Play** CD track 13.

**Texts mentioned:**

- The fall of the northern kingdom of Israel – 2 Kings 17.
- Jerusalem spared by miraculous intervention – 2 Kings 18:17 – 19:36 (especially 19:35,36).

**Read** Jonah 4

## Orientation 1

The basic story line of Jonah is probably among the top ten best known stories from the Bible. Even so, just make sure that people are familiar with the tail end of it by following through events in Jonah 3.

| | |
|---|---|
| Jonah 3:1–4 | Jonah goes to Nineveh and preaches. |
| Jonah 3:5,6 | The people respond to the message and repent. |
| Jonah 3:7–9 | The king also responds and orders a city-wide repentance, animals included. |
| Jonah 3:10 | God has compassion on the city, and spares it from punishment. |

## Investigation 1

1  What is the main 'message' of Jonah?

**Note:** As they'll hear in the audio clip, I think that the main thrust in Jonah comes in the final chapter. Jonah is about the audacity of God's forgiveness. God is more willing to forgive than we are, and sometimes greater faith can be found outside Israel (or the church) than in it.

2  How do you think the Israelites of the day would have responded to this message? Is this complimentary, or insulting?

3  Can we take Jonah's comments in 4:2 at face value? Are we

surprised to see that Jonah expected God to act with compassion towards a 'heathen' (ie non-Israelite) city?

## Preparation and Orientation 2

**Read** Nahum 1:1–15 (or 1:2–8)

Establishing the context for Nahum is more about ensuring the group know their Old Testament history. As always, judge for yourself how much of this background information the group will need.

These events all occurred at the time of the divided monarchy (well after David and Solomon):

- Nineveh was the capital city of the Assyrians.
- The Assyrians overran the northern kingdom, Israel (2 Kings 17).
- They virtually annihilated Jerusalem and Judah as well (2 Kings 18 – 19), but failed in the attempted siege of Jerusalem.
- The Book of Nahum probably comes from this period.
- The Assyrians in turn were overrun by the Babylonians and Medes (an event not recorded in the Bible).
- The Babylonians continued their campaign and were successful in their attack of Jerusalem and Judah (2 Kings 25).

## Investigation 2

4  Would it be fair to say that the bulk of the imagery here can be summarised in the words of verse 2? If so (and even if not), what is the phrase 'slow to anger' (verse 3) doing here?

5  If we compare Nahum 1:2,3 with Exodus 34:6,7 what do we learn from the changes that have been made to the standard refrain? Do those changes surprise us?

6  Who would have heard this prophecy? Would Nahum have travelled to Nineveh to deliver it, as Jonah did? Could this have been the text preached by Jonah?

**Note:** As mentioned in the **Leader's briefing**, it was very unusual for Israelite prophets to travel to other countries to deliver the message. It is far more likely that Nahum was a message for the Israelites to hear.

7  If this was a prophecy for the Judeans to hear, not the Assyrians, how (if at all) is our understanding of the phrase 'slow to anger' affected?

## Observation

**Play** CD track 14. Give the group a chance to ask any questions to clarify what they have just heard. When ready, move on.

**Text mentioned:**

- Jonah gives an eight-word-long message, with a 40-day warning – Jonah 3:4.

## Application

8   Who would be today's equivalent of the Assyrians? Al-Qaeda terrorists? Paedophiles? Economic immigrants?

9   What does it mean to leave room for God's vengeance?

10  Is there any place in the contemporary church for us to call on God to act in vengeance?

11  Have any group members ever been in situations where they feel God has 'shown them up'? Do we ever end up angry with God for his love and generosity?

12  Does Jonah demonstrate God's character of being 'slow to anger'? To what extent, then, should we demonstrate God's character?

13  Does God stop using us when we fail to act with his character?

### Summary

**Play** CD track 15.

**Texts mentioned:**

- Parable of the vineyard – Matthew 20:1–16
- Romans 5:8–10

## Adoration

- Read Romans 5:6–11. Offer prayers of thanksgiving to God that because Christ died for us while we were his enemies, we can have confidence in God's love for us now we are his friends.
- Sing or listen to a song or hymn that focuses on the sacrifice of Christ for us.

**Optional extra for next week:** encourage group members to compile a brief history of their experience of God on one side of A4 paper, charting and dating where possible the major landmarks of their faith journey.

# 6: REMEMBER THE LORD

## NEHEMIAH 9:17

### Leader's briefing

In Nehemiah 9 we move to an event that comes towards the end of the Old Testament period. With the people restored to the Promised Land from Babylon, Ezra and Nehemiah are trying to establish proper values and ethical behaviour in both them and the people who had remained in the land throughout the period of the exile.

We will be studying a prayer outlining Israelite history from the time of Abraham. We will see that God's actions and faithfulness are emphasised. In the midst of the passage comes the liturgical fragment we are studying: 'slow to anger' (Nehemiah 9:17).

In this session, the emphasis is twofold: first, on the spiritual value of re-calling God's actions; second, on the effect of hearing positive statements about God's character if our perception of him is different.

The **Application** section is quite demanding of time, so you should expect to move through the earlier **Investigation** fairly quickly.

### Preparation

**Play** CD track 16.

**Read** Nehemiah 9:13–21 (or 9:1–37).

### Orientation

You will need to decide just how far back in Nehemiah the group needs to go to establish the context for the reading. A good point to start from would be chapter 8, but you might prefer to look through the whole of Nehemiah. Let the group flick though the pages of their Bible as you give them the headlines:

| | |
|---|---|
| Nehemiah 1 | Nehemiah's prayer and concern for Jerusalem. |
| Nehemiah 2:1–9 | Nehemiah is commissioned to return to Jerusalem. |

| Nehemiah 2:10 – 7:3 | The rebuilding of the wall of Jerusalem, with some opposition. |
| Nehemiah 7:4–73 | A list of people who returned from Babylon. |
| Nehemiah 8:1–12 | Ezra reads the Law as the first stage in re-establishing Israelite religious practise and faith among the people. |
| Nehemiah 8:13–18 | The people celebrate the Festival of Booths, with more reading of the Law. |

## Investigation

1 The Israelites evidently made a point of recounting their history, recalling the things God had done for them in the past, and the ways they had failed him. What are the spiritual benefits of doing this?

**Note:** Several of the Psalms do something similar.

2 What effect does it have to give so little space in Nehemiah 9 to God's character and so much to his actions?

## Observation

**Play** CD track 17. Give the group an opportunity to ask questions to clarify what they have just heard. When ready, move on.

**Texts mentioned:**

– 'Remember and do not forget' – Deuteronomy 8:2,11,14,18.
– 'These commandments are to be upon your hearts' – Deuteronomy 6:6–8.

## Application

3 Do we make enough of our past history with God? Do you keep a diary or occasional journal and, if so, does it help you keep a broader picture of the way God works in your life?

Now is the time for group members who compiled a brief history of their faith journey to share from this experience, either in the whole group or in twos or threes. Be cautious about the time allocated to this, as it could easily dominate the whole discussion. Instead, concentrate on what the impact was on people of recording this history of God's involvement in their lives, and the way it affected their perception of God.

*If the group worked on a personal faith history:*

4 How much space, if any, did people give to a description of God's character as opposed to what he has done? If they did write about God's character, what did they write?

5 Did anyone include 'slow to anger'? If so, why?

6 If people did not include anything about God's character, do they feel their account would be improved by adding this?

*If the group did not complete a faith history:*

7 What is the benefit of including statements about God's character in a personal chronicle of God's activities in our lives, not restricting it to statements about what God has done?

8 What statements about God's character would people want to include if they did compile their own chronicle?

9 Would anyone include 'slow to anger'? If so, why? Or why not?

10 How distorted is our perception of past events? For example, do we automatically view every negative thing that has happened to us as God punishing us, and every positive thing as his blessing? Or do we view our own lives as something that happens without God's intervention? How would we go about establishing guidelines that would help us spot the way God is acting?

11 To what extent is our perception of what God has done in the past affected by our mood at the time when we think back on it? How can we overcome this problem?

12 In Nehemiah 9, some parts of Israelite history are skipped over with barely a mention. For example, the period of the monarchy gets minimal treatment in verses 29–31, with not a single king mentioned by name. In contrast, the exodus is described at length in verses 9–21. Why didn't they look harder for something to add from the period of the monarchy? Does that mean it is acceptable for us to pass over extended periods of our lives, saying that God was not overtly active during that period?

13 How would you summarise the benefits of compiling a personal history of God's actions in your life? When and how would it be of benefit to you to have such a chronicle to refer to?

14 What events would feature in a similar summary of your church's history with God?

## Summary

**Play** CD track 18.

## Adoration

Finish with:

– Sharing from people's individual chronicles (if not covered earlier), finishing each one by saying together something like, 'Thank you, Lord. Let us remember your love and goodness to us.'

– Or, short prayers of thankfulness for God's involvement in each person's life.

# 7: GREAT IS THE LORD

**PSALM 145:8**

### Leader's briefing

For our final session we return to Psalms once again for our last example of the phrase 'slow to anger'. That the phrase occurs again in the Psalms is in itself an indication of how important it was for Israelite worship. God's being slow to anger is praiseworthy. The God of the Israelites was different from the gods of the surrounding nations and that was cause for celebration. Without supporting evidence, it would be empty flattery to praise God for being slow to anger; the narrative passages give the basis for the claim, and translate it into opportunity for worship.

If Nehemiah 9, the passage for our previous session, concentrates on God's actions and says little about his character, Psalm 145 does quite the opposite. This psalm does not mention any of God's acts, though it does say that his 'mighty acts' will be spoken of and meditated on from generation to generation. But the dominant purpose of the text is extolling God. It is an upbeat 'good mood' psalm, one that does not consider the possibility of enemies or problems. This is a psalm for the sunny days in our lives.

So with this backdrop we will consider the tension that can result when our image of God is predominantly negative and fearful. These studies have focused on some very positive attributes of God's character. But, as we have already noted, there are those – perhaps not many, but some – who will struggle with this, who think of God more negatively, particularly in the guise of the 'celestial policeman'. Those with these preconceptions firmly established will be reluctant to believe this positive imagery, unable or unwilling to let go of what they believe to be true.

It can be difficult to open up about these things. In the company of other Christians who apparently seem to have no problems, we can be fearful of the reaction of others, should we admit to this sort of 'failure'.

Can I encourage you as group leader to foster a sense of safety and trust? One healthy way of facilitating this is by those who are more experienced and secure in their faith being willing to admit to having periods of doubt and struggle, and to testify to having moved on from some of these things. On the CD, I will personally admit to having had struggles with negative feelings about God over a two-year period; I hope that will encourage openness and honesty within the group.

That said, you cannot and must not force people to share what they do not want to share. As leader you, like the One you serve, have to be compassionate and gracious, slow to anger and abounding in love! Whatever is shared, ensure that no one is condemned or belittled for it, and that people are given the opportunity to receive prayer in response to anything they share.

Since this is the last session, it will be important to bring a sense of completeness and conclusion to the series. We have jumped from narrative to psalms to prophets and back to the psalms, concentrating on properly understanding each passage in itself. Hopefully the core phrase – 'slow to anger' – has not got lost en route. The opportunity to reflect on the series as a whole is an important and essential part of the process of integrating the sessions, and bringing to the fore whatever God has been particularly saying to individual group members.

## Preparation

**Play** CD track 19.

**Read** Psalm 145.

## Investigation

1  What things, if any, particularly stand out in Psalm 145 as encouragement for you?

2  We previously studied Psalms 86 and 103. How does the mood and tone of this psalm compare? Does this teach us anything about the mood we can be in when we want to remember that God is slow to anger?

3  If we compare Psalm 145:8 to Exodus 34:6–8 it is immediately apparent that a major portion of the original is missing. Are we right to pick and choose what we praise God for? Or is something different happening here?

## Observation

**Play** CD track 20. Give the group a chance to ask any questions to clarify what they have just heard. When ready, move on to **Evaluation**.

**Texts mentioned** (these are all texts previously studied):

- Exodus 34:6,7
- Numbers 14:17–19
- Psalms 86 and 103
- Nehemiah 9:17
- Jonah 4:2
- Nahum 1:3.

## Evaluation

4 A common (incorrect) image of God is that he is the 'celestial policeman', who has set up CCTV at every corner to catch us out in any and every sinful action and punish us for them swiftly. Is that (or has it been in the past) an issue for you?

**Note**: It is tempting to follow that question with the simplistic question, 'To what extent has this study series been a corrective to that viewpoint?' I leave it to you to respond to the way group members react and get them to consider it without the blunt question.

Since this is such a potentially emotive topic, do not be surprised if one or more group members admit to deep and long-held anguish due to fear of the policeman they view God to be. Be ready to offer prayerful encouragement and support, and to hold off from superficial answers.

5 How have group members freed themselves in the past from this or any other negative perceptions of God?

6 How do you achieve a healthy view of God which balances the 'slow to anger', loving God with the God who is holy and demanding of justice?

**Note:** This question has been considered before, but it may be appropriate to revisit as it's the last session. Feel free to omit.

## Application

7 Would anyone like to share what has emerged for them as the most important thing to take away from this series of studies?

## Summary

**Play** CD track 21.

**Texts mentioned:**

- 2 Peter 3:9
- The priestly blessing – Numbers 6:24–26.

## Adoration

Suggestions:

- Give thanks for any testimonies offered during the **Application** time.
- Sing a song or hymn that expresses the greatness of God.
- Pray for each other, particularly for the ongoing work of the Spirit in making God's truth known in each person.
- Close with repeating the blessing used on the final CD track: Numbers 6:24–26.

# 1: MOUNTAIN TOP ENCOUNTER

Reading: Exodus 34:1–9 (or 33:12 – 34:9 if you want a better sense of the background).

## Investigation

1    How do you feel as you read God's self-description in Exodus 34:6,7?

_____

_____

_____

2    Which part of the statement particularly resonates with you?

_____

_____

_____

3    Are you surprised to discover that the Old Testament describes God as 'slow to anger'? Does this fit your perception of God? Of the Old Testament?

_____

_____

_____

4    Which would you find most encouraging to your faith: a glimpse of God's glory (Exodus 33:18,23) or insight into an abstract theological statement of God's character (Exodus 34:6,7)? Why?

_____

5    So why does God explain himself in both ways?

_____

_____

_____

6    In Numbers 12:8 (among other places) we are told that Moses spoke with
     God 'face to face'. Exodus 33:20 states that even Moses cannot see God's
     face and live. How can this be consistent?

_____

_____

_____

**Optional extra questions**

7    In Exodus 32:9–13, Moses narrowly averts God's anger erupting against the
     people. Does this somehow invalidate the statement that God is 'slow to
     anger'? How do we maintain a coherent and rational statement about God's
     character?

_____

_____

_____

8      Looking at his actions in Exodus 32:19,20 and 32:25–28, would it be fair to say that Moses is 'slow to anger'? Does this affect our understanding of God as the one who is slow to anger?

_____

_____

_____

## Application

9      What would you include if asked to write your own 50-word description of God's character?

_____

_____

_____

10     Looking at God's self-description in Exodus 34, would you have had a similar balance between 'positive' and 'negative' aspects of God's character?

_____

_____

_____

11     If your summary would have been balanced differently, why?

_____

_____

_____

12    Which parts of your description are based on a theological statement about God? Which parts relate to your own experiences of God?

_____

_____

_____

13    What role (if any) do our past experiences of God play in forming our perception of who God is?

_____

_____

_____

**Optional extra questions**

If you attempted the optional questions in the Investigation section you might like to try the following:

14    To what extent should we emulate God as the One who is 'slow to anger'? Are we too much like Moses for it to be worth trying to develop a slow temper?

_____

_____

_____

_____

_____

# 2: THE WHOLE WICKED COMMUNITY

Reading: Numbers 14:1–25 (or 14:10–23)

## Investigation

1    Are you shocked by the speed with which God declares his intention to punish the people (verses 11,12)?

---

---

---

2    In verses 17 and 18 we see Moses confront God with his own declaration about his character that we studied from Exodus 34. Which of the following do you think is the best explanation for what is going on here?

– that God has forgotten how he is meant to behave and needs to be reminded? (In other words, if Moses had not said these things then God would have done what he declared he would do in verse 12.)

---

---

– that God is testing Moses, to see if he has learnt what God's true character is like?

---

---

– that prayer can change how God acts?

_____

_____

– a subtle combination of these options?

_____

_____

3    How should we interpret the phrase 'punishes the children for the sin of the fathers to the third and fourth generation' (verse 18)?

_____

_____

_____

4    In Numbers 14:20, the Lord declares that he has forgiven the people. Nevertheless, the passage continues with the information that the people will be punished. Is this consistent?

_____

_____

_____

5    Is there punishment for every sin we commit, even when we have asked for forgiveness? Or is this something that might only apply in certain situations?

_____

_____

_____

6    What similarities can you find between the situation in Numbers 14 and that in Exodus 32?

_____

_____

_____

7    What positive things can you spot in this passage, no matter how small they may be?

_____

_____

_____

## Evaluation

8    In the light of the punishment that results from the events surrounding these passages, is the claim that God is 'slow to anger' reasonable? Or empty and meaningless?

_____

_____

_____

9    What is your reaction to the observation that it is in the context of such widespread sin that the affirmation of this particular side of God's character is made?

_____

_____

_____

## Application

10    The sinful actions narrated in Exodus 34 and Numbers 14 are what we might call corporate sinfulness: the vast majority of the people fall into a sin. Are there any ways in which an entire local church can fall into corporate sinfulness?

11    In Numbers 14:11 and 14:23 God says that the people have treated him with contempt. What kind of thing might happen in a church today that might provoke God to view us in the same way, that we have treated him with contempt?

12    Are we – as Christians living after the crucifixion and the resurrection – somehow immune from punishment for such sin?

13    Are there occasions when we assume that our individual sinfulness warrants this level of response from God, even though it is nothing like the sort of sinfulness displayed by the Israelites?

14    What do these passages suggest about the contexts in which we might use such positive affirmations of God's character for ourselves?

_____

_____

_____

15    What of relevance do we learn from these passages about the phrase 'slow to anger' and the contexts in which it is used?

_____

_____

_____

# 3: HELP AND COMFORT

Reading: Psalm 86

## Investigation

1    Where and how do you imagine this psalm being used? Is it useful for congregational recitation? Or better used only by individuals?

2    Would you describe the imagery as innovative and creative? Or do you find it so full of stock phrases that you find it difficult to engage with? What are the implications of your verdict?

3    The psalmist spends more time praising God than talking about his problems. How realistic does this seem in the light of being 'poor and needy' (verse 1) and faced with 'the arrogant ... attacking' (verse 14)?

4 Who do you think are the 'arrogant', the 'band of ruthless men' and 'men without regard for you' (verse 14)? Do you need to identify them to be able to appreciate the psalm? Or is it actually better not to know?

_____

_____

_____

## Evaluation

5 Do you agree that in worship the familiar is encouraging and of greater comfort? Should worship make us feel comfortable?

_____

_____

_____

6 Is our worship or prayer (private or corporate) made more or less meaningful by the use of stock phrases?

_____

_____

_____

7 What other kinds of prayer can be meaningful and why?

_____

_____

_____

## Application

8     How often do we make space in our services for lament? Is it something to reserve for challenging national and international situations, like the World Trade Centre attacks of 11 September 2001, or the Indian Ocean Tsunami of Boxing Day 2004? Or something that should feature more regularly?

_____

_____

_____

9     What spiritual benefit might there be from incorporating lament into our services? What would that mean? What would we want to lament to God about?

_____

_____

_____

10    If this psalm models using general, non-specific terms to refer to a range of problems that people want to bring to God in prayer, can you come up with some contemporary parallel terms?

_____

_____

_____

11    Do our prayers show the balance of praise and petition seen in this psalm? If not, why not?

_____

_____

_____

# 4: AS FAR AS THE EAST IS FROM THE WEST

Reading: Psalm 103

## Investigation

1    Psalm 103 uses a variety of images drawn from nature: from the height of the heavens to the fragility of desert grass. Which images particularly resonate for you, and why?

_____

_____

_____

2    How much does this psalm rely on theologically sound statements in expressing God's character, and how much on poetic enthusiasm? Look, for example, at verse 10 and discuss its value. How far can we place our confidence in this and other verses in the psalm as objective truth to be trusted?

_____

_____

_____

3    Is there anything here that hints at the same sort of balance of character traits of God used in the Exodus and Numbers passages we studied?

_____

_____

_____

## Evaluation

4    Comparing Psalm 103:13,17; Exodus 34:7 and Numbers 14:18, do you agree that the psalm gives a different perspective on the narrative texts? Is it correcting them, expanding on them, or realigning them towards something bigger? Or do you think something different is happening?

## Application

5    What alternative images can you think of to express in contemporary terms Psalm 103:11,12 (or Isaiah 1:18)? If the group has already looked at some different translations or paraphrases of the psalm, that will help them with their response to this question. Do they find the examples inspiring? Or do they want to reject them as being too colloquial or dated?

Now use the **Exploring Psalm 103** sheet.

6    How do you feel about this sort of exercise? Which suggestions for new images particularly resonate with you? Does it help you to appreciate the biblical text better ?

7     Revelation 7:14 includes a somewhat bizarre image: robes washed in blood can come out white. What other ways are there of expressing the way that Jesus' death and resurrection has made forgiveness of sins possible?

_____

_____

_____

8     For some people, the image of God as a 'celestial policeman' is a very dominant one. This psalm celebrates a picture of God that is virtually the exact opposite of that. How can we achieve a balanced view of God, a healthy picture encompassing his mercy and his judgement?

_____

_____

_____

9     Compare the stock phrases of Psalm 86 with the creative imagery of Psalm 103. Which do you prefer and why?

_____

_____

_____

# 5: THE GOD WHO RELENTS

Readings: Jonah 4; Nahum 1:1–15

## Investigation 1

1   What is the main 'message' of Jonah?

_____

_____

_____

2   How do you think the Israelites of the day would have responded to this
    message? Is this complimentary, or insulting?

_____

_____

_____

3   Can we take Jonah's comments in 4:2 at face value? Are we surprised to see
    that Jonah expected God to act with compassion towards a 'heathen' (ie
    non-Israelite) city?

_____

_____

_____

## Investigation 2

4    Would it be fair to say that the bulk of the imagery here can be summarised in the words of verse 2? If so (and even if not), what is the phrase 'slow to anger' (verse 3) doing here?

_____

_____

_____

5    If we compare Nahum 1:2,3 with Exodus 34:6,7 what do we learn from the changes that have been made to the standard refrain? Do those changes surprise us?

_____

_____

_____

6    Who would have heard this prophecy? Would Nahum have travelled to Nineveh to deliver it, as Jonah did? Could this have been the text preached by Jonah?

_____

_____

_____

7    If this was a prophecy for the Judeans to hear, not the Assyrians, how (if at all) is our understanding of the phrase 'slow to anger' affected?

_____

_____

_____

## Application

8     Who would be today's equivalent of the Assyrians? Al-Qaeda terrorists? Paedophiles? Economic immigrants?

 

 

 

9     What does it mean to leave room for God's vengeance?

 

 

 

10     Is there any place in the contemporary church for us to call on God to act in vengeance?

 

 

 

11     Have any group members ever been in situations where they feel God has 'shown them up'? Do we ever end up angry with God for his love and generosity?

12  Does Jonah demonstrate God's character of being 'slow to anger'? To what extent, then, should we demonstrate God's character?

_____

_____

_____

13  Does God stop using us when we fail to act with his character?

_____

_____

_____

# 6: REMEMBER THE LORD

Reading: Nehemiah 9:13–21 (or 9:1–37)

## Investigation

1    The Israelites evidently made a point of recounting their history, recalling the things God had done for them in the past, and the ways they had failed him. What are the spiritual benefits of doing this?

_____

_____

_____

2    What effect does it have to give so little space in Nehemiah 9 to God's character and so much to his actions?

_____

_____

_____

## Application

3    Do we make enough of our past history with God? Do you keep a diary or occasional journal and, if so, does it help you keep a broader picture of the way God works in your life?

_____

_____

_____

*If the group worked on a personal faith history*:

4　　How much space, if any, did people give to a description of God's character as opposed to what he has done? If they did write about God's character, what did they write?

_____

_____

_____

5　　Did anyone include 'slow to anger'? If so, why?

_____

_____

_____

6　　If people did not include anything about God's character, do they feel their account would be improved by adding this?

_____

_____

*If the group did not write a faith history*:

7　　What is the benefit of including statements about God's character in a personal chronicle of God's activities in our lives, not restricting it to statements about what God has done?

_____

_____

_____

8    What statements about God's character would people want to include if they did compile their own chronicle?

_____

_____

_____

9    Would anyone include 'slow to anger'? If so, why? Or why not?

_____

_____

_____

10    How distorted is our perception of past events? For example, do we automatically view every negative thing that has happened to us as God punishing us, and every positive thing as his blessing? Or do we view our own lives as something that happens without God's intervention? How would we go about establishing guidelines that would help us spot the way God is acting?

_____

_____

_____

11    To what extent is our perception of what God has done in the past affected by our mood at the time when we think back on it? How can we overcome this problem?

_____

_____

_____

12    In Nehemiah 9, some parts of Israelite history are skipped over with barely a mention. For example, the period of the monarchy gets minimal treatment in verses 29–31, with not a single king mentioned by name. In contrast, the exodus is described at length in verses 9–21. Why didn't they look harder for something to add from the period of the monarchy? Does that mean it is acceptable for us to pass over extended periods of our lives, saying that God was not overtly active during that period?

13    How would you summarise the benefits of compiling a personal history of God's actions in your life? When and how would it be of benefit to us to have such a chronicle to refer to?

14    What events would feature in a similar summary of your church's history with God?

# 7: GREAT IS THE LORD

Reading: Psalm 145

## Investigation

1   What things, if any, particularly stand out in Psalm 145 as encouragement for you?

_____

_____

_____

2   We previously studied Psalms 86 and 103. How does the mood and tone of this psalm compare? Does this teach us anything about the mood we can be in when we want to remember that God is slow to anger?

_____

_____

_____

3   If we compare Psalm 145:8 to Exodus 34:6–8 it is immediately apparent that a major portion of the original is missing. Are we right to pick and choose what we praise God for? Or is something different happening here?

_____

_____

_____

## Evaluation

4    A common (incorrect) image of God is that he is the 'celestial policeman', who has set up CCTV at every corner to catch us out in any and every sinful action and punish us for them swiftly. Is that (or has it been in the past) an issue for you?

_____

_____

_____

5    How have group members freed themselves in the past from this or any other negative perceptions of God?

_____

_____

_____

6    How do you achieve a healthy view of God which balances the 'slow to anger', loving God with the God who is holy and demanding of justice?

_____

_____

_____

## Application

7    Would anyone like to share what has emerged for them as the most important thing to take away from this series of studies?

_____

_____

_____

# EXPLORING PSALM 103

Looking through the psalm, how can you 'translate' the expressions of God's character, particularly in verses 11–16, in ways that will be more readily recognisable to our own society?

Two examples of contemporary images:

- Though your sins be like motor-mechanic's fingers, they will be as clean as a newborn baby's.
- As thoroughly as Norton Utilities can securely wipe the information off your computer hard disk, so God has removed your sins from you.

Starter ideas:

- Washing and cleansing imagery: showering, shampooing…
- Bathroom and kitchen cleanliness: detergents, disinfectants…
- Medical imagery: antibiotics, vaccines…
- Technology: transport, astronomy, computers…
- Extremities: uncrackable codes, immovable objects…
- Really dirty things: muddy sports kit, rust…
- Things we'd rather not touch: mouldy peaches, a takeaway curry dropped in the street…
- The mess only little children create: painting with all the drips, a full nappy…

Your own images:

## DEEPER ENCOUNTER

- Bible study material for confident small groups
- Written by John Wilks, Director of Open Learning, London School of Theology
- 7 sessions in each book, with CD audio tracks and photocopiable worksheets

Other titles in this series:

**LOVE ONE ANOTHER** – So simple yet so profound; this command pervading John's letters and Gospel stretches us in our community life and helps us take a fresh look at our discipleship.

**PLAYING SECOND FIDDLE** – Our understanding of our faith will not flourish if we ignore the problems of real life. An exploration of Romans 12 gives us a valuable basis for establishing values and making decisions.

**KNOWING CHRIST CRUCIFIED** – A sacrificed lamb, a ransom for sin, a substitute for death, an appeaser of God's wrath; this study explores many of the Scriptural images which give deeper insights into why Jesus died.

Also recommended:

## ENCOUNTER WITH GOD

The ideal quarterly Bible reading guide for the thinking Christian who wants to interpret and apply the Bible in a way that is relevant to the issues of today's world. Daily comments from an international team of writers plus supporting features. Available from all Christian bookshops.

Please contact Scripture Union for a sample back issue to try with our compliments.

To ask for a sample, order or enquire about any of our publications:

- phone SU's mail order line: 0845 070 6006
- email info@scriptureunion.org.uk
- fax 01908 856020
- log on to www.scriptureunion.org.uk
- write to SU Mail Order, PO Box 5148, Milton Keynes MLO, MK2 2YX